RETIREE'S GUIDE TO MEDICARE

The book your insurance company does not want you to read

Retiree's Guide to Medicare

John Luo M.D. reserves all intellectual property rights including copyright.

John Luo M.D.
30 Quaker Ln Ste 35, Warwick RI 02886
Phone: 1-401-404-7373
Web: www.DoctorsChoiceUSA.com

Disclaimer:

The author, copyright owner, and publishers have made their best efforts to produce an informative book based on publically verifiable information. However, this book should not be construed as offering any personal, financial, medical, or legal advice.

Although all parties contributing to this book have made significant efforts to verify accuracy, things do change from time to time. The contributing parties, including the author, do not guarantee accuracy and are not responsible for any errors or any harm real or perceived otherwise.

FROM THE AUTHOR

I grew increasingly frustrated at the complexity of Medicare when I was going through my medical training. I was constantly asked questions by patients about Medicare and what plans to select.

Not knowing the answers, I started researching the different parts of Medicare in hopes of finding a better way to educate patients.

There is no shortage of information regarding Medicare. If you or any of your loved ones are turning 65, you are well aware of the barrage of mail from the government, insurance companies, and brokers all trying to "help you" – but possibly leaving you more confused.

I quickly realized that the key to understanding Medicare wasn't getting all the information, but rather focusing on the important facts first.

The purpose of this book is to help you understand the basics of Medicare, what big decisions you have to make, and what the typical situations look like.

This book does not go through the excruciating details of the Medicare system but rather organizes the important details most retirees need to know in order to make an educated decision. My goal is to create a simple guide that will work for most folks.

If you are an information junkie and just love debating about the differences between co-insurance and co-pays, then this book may be too elementary for you. However, if you're staring at retirement down the road and are wondering how you are going to navigate through the maze of Medicare, then hopefully you have found your guide.

As always, feel free to write to us with any questions or suggestions. I'd love to hear from you. Please visit us at www.DoctorsChoiceUSA.com

Sincerely,

John Luo M.D.
President

Doctor's Choice™

SPECIAL THANKS

I'm eternally grateful to have the companionship and love of my beautiful wife (and Chief Operating Officer) Leah, who reminds me every day that there's never been a better time in history to be successful doing what you love.

I'm also thankful for my son Orion, who taught me that the only way I'm going to be able to pay for his college is to deliver value to millions of people.

Thank you to my team, especially Al DeStefano, Pete Lucas, Carolyn Scharl, Max Bertman and Stephanie Arriaga for helping me with the contents of this version.

TABLE OF CONTENTS

SECTION 4: Common Situations   **75**

SECTION 5: Saving money   **96**

SECTION 1: Medicare Basics

This section will walk you through some of the basic terminologies in Medicare. Do not worry if you are not sure exactly how things fit together. We will cover that in Section 2.

1.1   What is Medicare?

Medicare is a federally subsidized program providing health insurance coverage for individuals who are 65 years old and older, or on disability.

In 1965, Lyndon B. Johnson signed Medicare into law as a way to provide health insurance for Americans 65 and older. Prior to Medicare, only 64% of Americans 65 and older had health insurance. Many were denied covered due to pre-existing conditions and those who were approved were paying upwards of 3 times the premium of someone half their age.

1.2 Who qualifies for Medicare?

Medicare is available to American citizens 65 and older, as well as individuals who have been disabled for 24 months.

Medicare may also be available to non-citizens under green card status who have lived in the United States for more than 5 years.

Individuals suffering from certain diseases such as End Stage Renal Disease (ESRD) or Lou Gehrig's (ALS) qualify for Medicare based on disease.

1.3   What are the different parts?

There are 5 major parts of Medicare:

Part A – covers hospitalization

Part B – covers outpatient services

Part C – Medicare Advantage, a plan that combines hospital, outpatient, and often prescription coverage into an all-in-one plan administered by private insurance companies.

Part D – covers prescriptions

Medigap – supplemental plan offered by private insurance companies to fills in the gaps not covered by Parts A and B.

1.4   What is Part A?

Part A covers hospitalization in addition to:

- Skilled nursing facility care

- Hospice

- Home health services

For most individuals, there is no monthly cost for

Part A. You have paid for Part A through payroll

taxes for Medicare. Most individuals are required

to pay 40 quarters (10 years) of Medicare taxes in

order to be eligible for Part A at no cost.

Part A comes with a deductible of $1,340 (for 2018). This deductible is per "benefit period." Each benefit period is each time you are hospitalized and ends 60 days after discharge. This means that if you were hospitalized and are readmitted within 60 days of discharge for a similar condition, it counts as the same benefit period and you will not have to pay another deductible. After 60 days, any admission requires another deductible.

Most individuals enroll in Part A when they turn 65 with the Social Security offices.

1.5   What is Part B?

Part B covers outpatient services including doctor's visits, imaging, labs, outpatient surgery, and certain medications administered only by healthcare professionals. Part B comes with a $183 (2018) annual deductible. After the deductible, services are covered at 80%.

For most individuals, Part B starts at a monthly cost of $134 per person per month (2018 rates). Rates are higher for individuals making over $85,000 (filing single) or $170,000 (filing joint). Please see the table below for Part B premium surcharge based on income.

Yearly income in 2016 (for what you pay in 2018)			You pay (in 2018)
File individual tax return	File joint tax return	File married & separate tax return	
$85,000 or less	$170,000 or less	$85,000 or less	$134.00
above $85,000 up to $107,000	above $170,000 up to $214,000	Not applicable	$187.50
above $107,000 up to $133,500	above $214,000 up to $267,000	Not applicable	$267.90
above $133,500 up to $160,000	above $267,000 up to $320,000	Not applicable	$348.30
above $160,000	above $320,000	above $85,000	$428.60

Most individuals enroll in Part B when Medicare becomes their primary source of health insurance. For individuals working past 65, signing up for Part B may not be necessary if an employer plan is still in effect. We suggest you contact your human resource department to see whether Part B is necessary if you're still employed. Rules can be different for different size companies.

1.6   What is Part C?

Part C (Advantage plans) are privately run

Medicare plans by companies, such as United

Health and Blue Cross, and are subsidized by the

federal government. Advantage plans often

provide an all-in-one package including inpatient,

outpatient, and prescription coverage.

Medicare Advantage plans are required to cover all

benefits included with original Medicare, but can

also offer additional benefits above and beyond

original Medicare.

Advantage plans have out of pocket expenses such as co-pays, co-insurances, as well as limitations on which providers or hospitals a member can visit (network restrictions).

Advantage plans can potentially offer a lower monthly premium and a yearly out of pocket maximum in exchange for co-pays and network restrictions.

An individual must be enrolled in Parts A + B and continue to pay Part B premiums in order to enroll in an Advantage plan.

1.7   What is Part D?

Unlike most Advantage plans, Supplemental Plans do not include prescription coverage. An individual must purchase a stand-alone Part D Prescription Plan in addition to their Supplemental plan.

Part D prescription plans come with out of pocket expenses such as co-pays, deductibles, and a coverage gap also known as the "donut hole." Co-pays and deductibles are often based on the type of drug categorized by tiers with generics being the least expensive and brand name or specialty medications being the more expensive prescriptions.

1.8   What is the Donut Hole?

The coverage gap (donut hole) affects individuals with high drug costs. When an individual's drug costs reach $3,750 (2018), the donut hole starts and for the most part, drug costs will be higher (approximately 35% of full cost of brand names for 2018). After drug costs reach a catastrophic amount ($5,000 for 2018), costs will decrease significantly until the following calendar year.

- Your plan covers you with co-pays up to $3750 in total drug costs

Stage 1 (initial)

Stage 2 (Coverage gap/donut hole)

- After $3750, you pay 35% cost of brand name I 44% cost of generic drugs

- After you pay $5,000 for the calendar year, you pay greater of $3.35 generic and $8.35 name brand or 5% for the rest of the year (resets Jan 1)

Stage 3 (Catastrophic)

1.9   What is Medigap?

Medigap (Supplemental) plans supplement Parts A and B. Supplemental plans are standardized based on letters A-N in 47 states. Each plan provides different levels of coverage for out of pocket expenses not covered by Parts A and B.

Certain Supplemental Plans can cover 100% of the costs associated with Parts A and B, leaving no expenses such as co-pays, deductibles, or co-insurance when visiting the doctor or hospital. Supplemental plans also allow individuals to visit any doctor or hospital in the country that accepts Medicare without the need for referrals.

Supplemental Plans can be seen as "all you can eat" where an individual is trading a higher monthly premium in exchange for minimal out of pocket expenses and flexibility of providers. Individuals must enroll in Parts A and B in order to enroll in a Supplemental Plan.

SECTION 2: Getting to the Meat and Potatoes (or Kale and Potatoes if you're vegan)

This section highlights how the various parts of Medicare work together and your one big decision. There is no universally perfect option for a person, but there are typically plans to fit your exact needs if you understand the key factors.

2.1 How do all the parts work together?

In section 1, we went over the ABCDs of

Medicare. Now I'd like you to forget about

everything you've read (not hard right?)

All joking aside, I find that most individuals get

caught up on the ABCDs and miss how the parts

work together.

Full Medicare coverage works in two ways:

1. Part A + Part B + Medigap (Supplemental

Plan) **+ Part D**

Over half of Americans on Medicare fall under this

category (source: kff.org).

Part A covers hospitalization, Part B covers

outpatient services, Medigap supplements most or

all (depending on the plan) costs associated with

Parts A + B, and Part D covers prescriptions.

2. Part C (Advantage)

About a third of Americans choose an Advantage

plan which combines hospital, outpatient, and

often times prescription coverage in an all-in-one

plan administered by a private insurance company.

You still have to be enrolled in Parts A + B of

Medicare and pay your Part B premiums to enroll

in Part C.

2.2 Your one big decision

As you may have guessed by now, your big decision isn't with the ABCDs but rather picking between a Supplemental + Part D plan versus an Advantage plan.

There is no universally correct choice and the options differ based on your location and needs.

There are three main factors behind your decision between a Supplemental + Part D plan and an Advantage plan.

These three factors are:

1. Your health

Do you visit the doctor once a week, every month, once or year, or somewhere in between? Do you have any procedures coming up or are you frequently hospitalized?

2. Your lifestyle

Are you staying mostly local for your care or do you plan on living in multiple states throughout the year?

3. Your financial situation

Did you budget for healthcare expenses or are you in a situation where any cost would be a financial strain?

2.3 Who enrolls in a Supplemental + Part D Plan?

With a supplemental plan, you can visit any doctor or hospital in the entire country that takes Medicare with no referrals needed. Depending on the plan, your co-pays and deductibles could be covered up to 100%. In other words, you will not have to pay out of pocket when you use Medicare approved services.

Overall, supplemental plans give you robust coverage with national flexibility.

Supplemental Plans are a great fit for individuals who have frequent medical needs, individuals looking to minimize unexpected medical bills or those who travel or live in different parts of the country for months at a time.

Again, with a supplemental plan, you'll need to pick up a separate Part D prescription plan.

2.4 How do you pick a Supplemental Plan?

Supplemental plans are standardized in 47 states by letters A through N.

What this means is that Plan A from company 1 covers exactly the same as Plan A from company 2.

The best method to pick a supplemental plan is to choose the plan that fits your needs, and then select the company that has the lowest premium. (It's also important to take a look at the stability of a company by looking historical increases to make sure that a low price today doesn't mean high increases down the road).

The most common plans we recommend are Plans F, G, and N.

Plan F covers costs associated with A + B at 100%. This means no co-pays or deductibles at the doctor or hospital. It is not hard to see why Plan F is a popular plan.

However, it is also typically the most expensive. Individuals turning 65 after 2020 will no longer be able to sign up for Plan F due to the Medicare Access and CHIP Reauthorization Act (MACRA). However, individuals who are on the plan will be grandfathered in. The alternative is Plan G.

Plan G has the same coverage as Plan F except it does not cover the Part B deductible ($183 for 2017). You'll pay for the first $183 in outpatient costs and then the plan picks up 100% after that. Plan G is still a very robust option. It makes sense to choose plan G versus Plan F if Plan G will save you more than $183/year in premiums.

Plan N covers you for the big costs such as outpatient surgery, nursing home, and hospitalization. However, you're responsible for the Part B deductible, $20 co-pays at the doctors, and $50 co-pays at the emergency room. Plan N also does not cover Part B surcharges. In cases where providers do not take Medicare assignment (does not agree to take what Medicare pays them), providers can still accept Medicare patients, but are permitted to bill the patient an extra 15% on top of what Medicare allows. Plan F and G cover these surcharges but Plan N does not.

Under the Medicare Overcharge Measure Law (MOM), it is illegal for providers to bill patients for excess charges in Connecticut, Massachusetts, Minnesota, New York, Ohio, Pennsylvania, Rhode Island and Vermont.

Plan N is a great way to protect against big costs such as outpatient procedures and hospitalizations while maintaining a modest premium.

Some insurance companies increase premiums as you age while some companies base premiums off of a geographical region regardless of age. Make sure you're aware of the premium increases and that they are affordable for you as you age.

2.5 How do you pick a Part D Plan?

Picking the right Part D plan can be a difficult process. On average, there are over 20 different plans in each state. Each plan can have a different monthly premium, different formulary (what drugs are covered), different co-pays for each drug, and different prices for each drug at each pharmacy (which will affect your coverage gap calculations).

All of this will drive you nuts.

To keep it simple, you will only need 2 pieces of information to start your search: what drugs you take and what pharmacy you use.

The government has put together a great website: Medicare.gov to help you with prescription costs.

On the website, you can enter your prescriptions and preferred pharmacy and it will tell you which plan will save you the most money through either picking up your prescriptions at the pharmacy or by mail order.

Each plan is not only listed by what your prescriptions costs are but also by star rating. Medicare rates plans based on stars. Similar to restaurants, 1 star is the lowest and 5 stars are the highest. Star ratings are based on a complex series of criteria including patient satisfaction, number of errors, and complaints. We typically recommend a plan with at least a 3 star rating.

Also, be aware that plans can change on January 1st of each year. It's wise to look at your options between October 15 and December 7 (the annual enrollment period – more on this later) to make sure that your current plan will still fit your needs next year.

You can also talk to someone at Medicare to enroll by calling 1-800-MEDICARE.

2.6 Who typically enrolls in an Advantage Plan?

Unlike Supplemental plans, Advantage plan benefits can vary significantly between plans. All plans have to cover at least what Medicare covers in terms of services. However, plans can add additional benefits such as annual eye exams, vision hardware allowances, gym memberships, and dental (plus more). Each plan can have different co-pays for services and most plans will include prescription coverage as well.

The biggest benefits of an Advantage plan are the monthly premiums and extra benefits on top of what Medicare covers. The monthly premiums are typically much lower than a supplemental plan.

However, as mentioned before, Advantage plans often come with higher out of pocket costs as well as network restrictions on who you can see as a provider versus Supplemental plans.

Advantage plans are typically fit for individuals who are reasonably healthy, do not regularly travel out of state, and do not mind paying for medical services if it means a lower monthly cost.

2.7 How do you pick an Advantage Plan?

Different advantage plans are available in different states. Sometimes, even different counties within the same state can have different plan offerings.

There are 3 main factors to check off your list when choosing an Advantage plan.

1. Providers

Make sure that your preferred physicians, hospitals, and facilities are part of the network. Understand whether a plan requires referrals and whether there is an out of network option.

2. Prescriptions

Make sure that all of your prescriptions are covered as well as understand their costs. Unlike the Supplemental + Part D route, you cannot choose another prescription plan when enrolling in an advantage plan. You have to stay with the option that's bundled into the plan.

3. Price

Advantage plans can start at $0/month. This means that you only pay your Part B premium.

Even though some plans do not cost you any more on a monthly basis, the insurance companies get an additional payment from Medicare for having you as a member of the plan.

2.8 What does Medicare not cover?

Although some Advantage plans may include
additional benefits, Medicare typically does not
cover the following:

1. Dental

This is the number one benefit asked for in regards
to Medicare. Medicare does not cover routine
cleanings/exams, or any services typically covered
by traditional dental insurance. However,
Medicare will cover you for oral-facial surgery in
the event that it is related to your overall health
(e.g. cancer). Some Advantage plans may include
basic dental benefits.

Many individuals choose to either pay cash at the dentist or purchase an individual dental plan from a dental insurance carrier.

2. Vision

Medicare typically does not cover routine eye exams or give you an allowance for vision hardware. However, some Advantage plans may add these benefits as part of their plan.

3. Skilled nursing facilities past 100 days

Medicare will pay for up to 100 days in a skilled nursing facility. This is typically for individuals recovering after hospitalization. This is a temporary step before returning home. After 100 days, your long-term care insurance comes in if you have one.

Low-income individuals may qualify for state assistance or Medicaid, which could offset the cost of a nursing home.

4. Hearing aids

Medicare typically does not cover hearing aids. However, some Medicare Advantage plans may offset the cost of hearing aids via a discount program or as a direct benefit.

5. Spouses

Medicare plans are individual policies. Unfortunately if a spouse is under 65 or if a Medicare eligible individual has dependents, Medicare will not cover them. Spouses and dependents that do not qualify for Medicare will have to consider COBRA, insurance available through employment/school, or a plan directly from a health insurance company or health insurance exchange.

2.9 Can I change my plans?

Most individuals will have the opportunity to switch plans each year.

For Advantage and Part D prescription plans, individuals will be able to evaluate and switch plans during the annual enrollment period between October 15 – December 7th. Changes become effective January 1st of the following year.

For Supplemental Plans, individuals can switch each month. However, depending on the state and company, there may be underwriting (meaning that you could be denied or subject to increased premiums due to health) or have a waiting period (a period of time where pre-existing conditions are not covered).

Individuals can also qualify for Special Election Periods (SEP) during the year, allowing them to switch plans outside of AEP. Common SEPs include moving, loss of employer coverage, low-income subsidy, Medicaid eligibility, etc. (more on this in Section 3).

SECTION 3: When and How

Section 3 highlights the most common reasons to enroll in Medicare, as well as the mechanics behind when to do what.

3.1 Three common reasons to enroll in Medicare

Most individuals fall into three different categories when enrolling in Medicare.

1. Turning 65 – becoming eligible for Medicare via age

2. Retiring after 65 –leaving employer insurance

3. Disability – under 65 and disabled for 24 months

Others may qualify through disease such as End Stage Renal Disease and Lou Gehrig's (ALS).

3.2 Turning 65

Turning 65 is the most common reason most individuals enroll in Medicare. You can sign up for Medicare as early as 3 months before your 65th birthday and as late as 3 months after (for a 7 month window).

The earliest that Medicare coverage can start is the 1st of the month of your 65th birthday. For example, if your birthday was July 14th, then the earliest Medicare can start is July 1st. (For individuals with birthdays on the first the month, Medicare will start the month before).

If you are signing up for Medicare when you turn 65 and Medicare will be your only source of health insurance, then you would have to sign up for both Parts A and B.

You can sign up for Parts A and B through the social security offices either in person, over the phone, or online at ssa.gov/medicare.

You can sign up for Medicare independent of collecting social security benefits.

However, if you are already collecting social security benefits before your 65th birthday, you will automatically be enrolled in Medicare and will receive your Medicare card in the mail indicating when your Part A and Part B will start.

After you have received your Medicare card showing that you have signed for Parts A + B, you can enroll in a Supplemental, Advantage, or a Part D prescription plan.

It typically takes 2-3 weeks to receive your Medicare card after signing up and another 2-3 weeks for your Advantage, Supplemental, or Part D prescription plan cards. Please plan accordingly. We recommend starting the process at least 3 months before you need coverage to begin.

3.3 Retiring after 65

1 in 5 Americans are working past 65. If you are one of those individuals, then there are some additional steps you will need to take to make sure that you are in the right place.

If you are currently enrolled in a group health insurance plan offered by your employer, you have the option to remain on the plan. Your employer cannot force you to go on Medicare or drop you from the plan for any reason (as long as you continue to meet the plan's eligibility criteria). However, you are free to choose to go on Medicare if it is going to be a better deal for you.

Many group health insurance plans have recently adopted higher deductibles in addition to higher co-payments and co-insurance levels. The premiums are also steadily increasing, so it is likely your employee contributions are rising as well. (This is the amount you pay each month for coverage, usually via payroll deduction).

Given these factors, it is wise to thoroughly consider your options when you turn 65. Many Medicare plans (even the least expensive Medicare Advantage Plans) usually offer no deductibles and several other benefits.

For individuals wishing to stay on their employer plan after 65 due to lower cost, robust benefits, or the need to cover dependents, you may not need to sign up for Medicare. If you work for a small company (less than 20 total employees), Medicare is considered your primary insurance (meaning Medicare pays first for covered services). You should consult your human resources department or current insurance carrier regarding coordination of benefits.

Most individuals sign up for Part A (because it has no monthly premium) and forgo Part B until retirement.

You can sign up for Part A only with the social security offices.

If you have been automatically enrolled in Part B, you can also choose to deny Part B by filling out the back of your Medicare card or contacting the social security office.

When you are ready to retire, you can enroll in Part B. You will need to fill out form CMS40B to indicate that you want to enroll in Part B. Your employer will need to fill out form CMS-L564 to indicate that you are leaving work coverage and you have had creditable coverage from the time you were 65 to your retirement in order to avoid any penalties. These forms can be requested through the Social Security offices or by visiting them at SSA.gov

Leaving your employer's coverage opens a special election period for you to enroll in Medicare during the year. Enrolling in Part B will open a special election period for you to select an Advantage, Supplemental, and Part D plan.

3.4 Disability

If you are disabled and collecting social security disability benefits, you will automatically be enrolled in Medicare when you have collected benefits for 24 months.

In most states, it can be difficult to enroll in a supplemental plan if you are under 65. However, you will be eligible for an Advantage plan (except in cases of End Stage Renal Disease) or a stand alone Part D Plan.

3.5 Avoiding Penalties

Medicare assesses a 10% a year penalty for Part B and a 1% a month penalty for Part D. This amount is tagged onto your monthly premium when you do enroll in Part B or Part D, and will continue for the rest of your life.

The general rule of thumb is that if you were covered by a creditable active employee health insurance plan, then you will not be penalized for signing up late.

The purpose of this rule is the make sure that everyone pays into the insurance system.

If you qualified for Medicare under the age of 65 due to disability and you did not enroll in Part D, any penalties incurred will reset to $0 when you turn 65.

3.6 Reviewing your options yearly

Each year, your plan could change. October 15 to December 7th is the Medicare Annual Enrollment Period (AEP). This is the time when plans for next year are revealed. Individuals on Medicare will have the option to evaluate changes and switch plans if necessary.

During AEP, individuals can change their Part D or Advantage plans, as well as switch from a standalone Part D plan to an Advantage Plan and vice versa.

If you are switching between Advantage or Part D plans, your previous plan will be automatically cancelled on 12/31. If you are switching from a Supplemental + Part D plan to an Advantage plan, your Part D will automatically be cancelled but you will need to notify your Supplemental plan company to end your coverage as of 12/31.

Unfortunately, plan changes are buried in thick booklets from the insurance companies and rarely get read by consumers.

It is extremely important to review changes to your current plan for next year to make sure that there are no surprises come January 1st. **Your current insurance company is required to send you an**

updated Evidence of Benefits (EOB) for next year's plan in early October.

The three major changes to evaluate on an Advantage plan are:

1. Changes in network

Your doctors may be in your plan this year, but there is no guarantee that they will participate in it next year. Be sure to check that all your doctors are in next year's plan. If your doctors are not, then be prepared to either find new doctors or find another plan.

2. Changes to formulary

Check to make sure that your prescriptions are still

covered and that the costs are acceptable to you.

Be sure to shop around for better deals.

This is especially true with standalone Part D

prescription plans.

3. Changes to co-pays and premiums

Plans can raise or drop their premiums and co-pays

each year. Be sure that you are aware of any

changes so you can budget accordingly.

Supplemental plan benefits typically do not

change. The only thing that changes is the

monthly premium based on cither your area or

your age. If the prices are acceptable, most individuals will just stay on their current supplemental plan. The most common reason for individuals to switch plans, in our experience, has been when the premiums are too high.

If you switch from a supplemental plan to another supplemental plan, be sure to check whether the plan you are switching into requires underwriting. If so, it would be wise to keep your current supplemental plan until your enrollment in your new plan is confirmed.

3.7 What if my circumstances change?

One of the biggest concerns is "if I pick a plan based on my needs today, will I be stuck in it forever?"

The short answer is no.

As we discussed in the last section, each year you will have the opportunity to evaluate your Medicare Advantage and Part D prescription options and switch plans during AEP.

However, if your circumstances change during the year, you may qualify for a special election period to enroll in another plan.

The most common changes in circumstance include:

Moving

If you are moving to a location outside of your plan's coverage area, you will have an opportunity to switch plans. If you tell your plan before you move, then your window to switch begins the month before you move and ends 2 months after you move.

If you tell your plan after you have moved, then your window begins the month you tell your plan and lasts two more months after that.

Qualifying for low income subsidies or Medicaid

If you qualify for low-income subsidies or Medicaid based on income/assets, you will have the opportunity to switch plans during the year. Medicaid eligible individuals (duals) can switch plans each month on a rolling basis.

Being admitted to a nursing home

If you are in a nursing facility or a long-term care hospital, you can switch plans each month. Your plans can be switched within 2 months after leaving the institution.

For a full list of special enrollment periods, visit https://www.medicare.gov/sign-up-change-plans

3.8 Health savings accounts

Many employers are moving toward qualified
High Deductible Health Plans (HDHP) with a
Health Savings Account (HSA). HSAs allow
employees to contribute a portion of their income
tax free into an account to pay for qualified health
expenses. Any unused funds roll over each year
and stay with the employee after retirement.

When someone enrolls in Medicare (including Part
A only), they are no longer allowed to contribute
to their HSA. However, they may still take tax-free
distributions for qualified health expenses.

Individuals can also withdraw money for non-medical expenses after 65 without any penalties (though these distributions are not considered tax free).

If your employer offers an HSA plan and you would like to stay on your employer plan, do not sign up for Part A when you turn 65.

When you are ready to retire and go on Medicare, you must stop contributing to your HSA 6 months before you apply for Social Security benefits since Medicare Part A enrollment will be backdated by 6 months (provided you were eligible).

Since you cannot make HSA contributions while you are enrolled in Part A, you may incur taxes on any amounts deposited during this 6-month period.

Please also note that you cannot pay for your Supplemental Plan premiums through your HSA.

3.9 COBRA

COBRA (Consolidated Omnibus Budget Reconciliation Act) allows eligible employees, spouses, or dependents to continue their group coverage after separation of employment and be offered the same coverage(s) they had while active on the employer plan.

However, individuals will be responsible for paying up to 102% of the cost (the full monthly premium, plus an administrative fee). This makes the COBRA option potentially very expensive.

Most individuals eligible for Medicare will elect to go on Medicare immediately after their employer plan ends and will not elect COBRA.

However, if they have a spouse under 65 or dependents who need coverage, COBRA could be an attractive option. The current plan may offer greater benefits or a lower price than what is available to the general public.

COBRA typically extends coverage for 18 months but could potentially be extended to 36 months depending on special situations. For exact details of what your COBRA plan will entail, please consult your human resources department.

SECTION 4: Common Situations

Medicare can be conceptually difficult to understand. When put into the context of real life situations – how the pieces work together can become much more clear. Here are the 9 most common scenarios we run into.

4.1 "I'm healthy and stay local"

"Joe is a 67 year old retiring from a local

University where he has worked for over 30 years.

He has lived in the same state his whole life. He

exercises regularly and is on two generic

maintenance medications for his blood pressure

and cholesterol.

He visits his primary care doctor 1-2 times a year,

his eye doctor every year, and his dermatologist

for a regular checkup. He does not mind paying

co-pays if it means a lower monthly premium.

Joe plans on taking week long trips to see his

grandkids out of state, but does not have any plans

to live in other parts of the country."

In Joe's situation, he is healthy and stays local.

We would suggest that he consider an Advantage

plan since he does not frequently use medical

services. The amount of money he will save on

monthly premiums over a supplemental plan will

be greater than the cost of his co-pays.

Key points for Joe to consider when choosing an

Advantage plan are the co-pays (especially for

outpatient surgery/hospitalization) as well as

whether his doctors are in the network. He will be

able to put the monthly difference in his savings

for a rainy day (or spend it).

4.2 "I'm healthy, but I don't want any big medical bills"

"Karen is a 68 year old looking at retirement in the next 2 years. She considers herself healthy and lives an active lifestyle. She visits her primary care doctor and routine specialists for checkups. However, she is concerned about a family history of cancer and does not want any large medical bills."

Karen's situation is the common "I'm healthy today, but I don't know what's in store for the future." For Medicare Advantage plans, the costliest services are typically for inpatient hospitalization and outpatient procedures.

Since certain insurance companies (depending on state) will require underwriting if Karen wants to go on a Supplemental plan more than 6 months after her Part B starts, it may be wise for Karen to start on a Supplemental + Part D plan. Supplemental plans will cover her for all the big costs such as inpatient hospitalization and outpatient procedures. Once she is enrolled in a Supplemental Plan, the insurance company cannot deny coverage or raise rates based on health as long as Karen continues to pay her monthly premiums. Depending on Karen's risk tolerance, she also may be suitable for an Advantage plan that has reasonable out of pocket expenses.

4.3 "I'm healthy and will live in multiple states"

"Bob is 65 and retired. He spends his winters in Florida and the rest of his year in Rhode Island. He's healthy with just an annual checkup and the occasional sick visit. However, he has a primary care doctor in RI and a primary doctor in Florida just in case."

In Bob's situation, flexibility in terms of network and a plan without the need for referrals could be important. Many Advantage plans are HMO plans, meaning that you have to designate one primary care physician who provides referrals for specialists.

Given Bob's situation, he would most likely be better served by a Supplemental plus a Part D plan due to a wider network and no need for referrals. He will be able to electively go to any doctor and hospital that takes Medicare.

If Bob's budget does not allow for a supplemental plan, then an Advantage plan without referrals with out of network benefits (often times called Point-of-Service) may be a good option.

Some Advantage plans may offer unique travel benefits as well, allowing members to activate a network of doctors around them when they travel.

Again, each Advantage plan can be different so be sure to ask about out of network benefits if they are important to you.

4.4 "I have medical conditions and I stay local"

"Gertrude is 74 and has lived in the same town for the past 20 years. She is retiring from a local non-profit after 40 years of service. She has high blood pressure, a thyroid condition that her physician is monitoring, and goes to the doctor every quarter."

Given that Gertrude stays local and frequently has office visits, she may not necessarily need a Supplemental plan. An Advantage plan with low co-pays for office visits with all of her doctors in the network could fit her well and allow her to put some money away.

However, if Gertrude is concerned about potentially high medical bills down the road, she may want to consider a "Select" Supplemental Plan if one is available in her area. Select Supplemental plans can come with a network of hospitals but will typically cover most or all out of pocket expenses in that particular network. This works well for someone with high medical costs but stays local. Premiums will be significantly less than a non-Select Supplemental plan with the same level of coverage.

4.5 "I've got a few medical conditions and I travel"

"Tim is 70. He has a home in Connecticut, New York, and Arizona. He suffers from prostate cancer, has had a history of heart conditions, and is pre-diabetic. He knows that if any medical issues should arise, he would prefer to seek out doctors in Boston or New York."

Tim would be a candidate for a Supplemental + Part D drug plan since he prefers to see providers in different states electively and most likely will have medical procedures in the future.

4.6 "I'm constantly in and out of the hospital"

"Betty is 71, retiring from work, and has several medical conditions such as COPD, diabetes, and a history of stroke. She regularly sees her primary care doctor as well as 5 specialists. She visits the doctor almost every month. Unfortunately for Betty, she often suffers from COPD exacerbations and has regular inpatient hospital stays."

In Betty's situation, the likely option would be a robust Supplemental plan (Plan F or G) given her medical history. Her savings at the doctor will most likely outweigh her monthly premium. She would then need to choose a Part D plan which fits

her prescriptions.

4.7 "I've got a few big procedures coming up"

"Steve is 65 and looking forward to retirement. His current employer plan has a high deductible and his surgeon recently recommended a knee replacement. Smitty is looking forward to Medicare and getting a plan with little or no out of pocket expenses. He is other wise in average health with a few maintenance medications."

In Smitty's case, a Supplemental + Part D drug plan would mostly likely fit his immediate situation. Given that supplemental plans F, G, and N cover hospital stays as well as outpatient surgeries at 100%, Smitty would save a significant amount of money over his current employer plan.

Since he is retiring from work and signing up for

Part B, his enrollment into a Supplemental plan is

guaranteed within the 6 months of his Part B

effective date.

He can choose to switch to an Advantage plan the

following AEP should he decide that a

Supplemental plan would be too expensive.

4.8 "My prescription costs are too high"

"June is 70 and has several chronic conditions that are well managed by her primary care physician. She visits her doctors every quarter and has 15 different prescriptions, 3 of which are brand name."

Less than 10% of individuals on Medicare fall into the donut hole. However, for those who do, the costs can be astronomical. As a recap, Medicare covers up to $3,700 of prescriptions (that's the full retail cost of your prescriptions). Within the $3,700, you're paying your deductible (if your plan has one) and co-pays. Your insurance company is paying the remainder. When total drug costs cross over $3,700, you fall into the donut

hole, where you're responsible for 45% of the cost

of your brand name drugs and 68% of your

generics.

Unfortunately in June's situation, there is no

"Cadillac" drug plan. Almost all the plans

available to her will have the donut hole and given

that she takes three brand name medications, her

out of pocket expenses are likely going to be high

regardless of which route she takes.

Instead of focusing on Advantage versus

Supplemental + Part D, individuals in June's

situation should factor in the estimated yearly cost

of their prescriptions and weigh which plan will give the most discounts on prescriptions.

June may also look into prescription discount programs, available low-income assistance, as well as any pharmaceutical grants to offset the costs of her medications (more on this in Section 5).

4.9 "My spouse is under 65"

"Rodney is 72 and is retiring from work. His wife is 63 and does not qualify for Medicare. Rodney is healthy and does not travel much. He is leaning towards an Advantage plan. However, he is concerned about coverage for his wife."

This is a very common situation. We all cannot marry our high school sweethearts. For spouses where one is over 65 and one is under, the spouse under 65 will have to get an individual policy to cover their medical needs. There are 3 main ways a spouse under 65 can get coverage:

1. COBRA

As mentioned in Section 3, COBRA continues the current employer plan for typically up to 18 months at full cost plus an administrative fee to the policyholder. Individuals typically choose this option if the benefits offered by the employer fits their needs better than any other option or if they do not qualify for less expensive coverage.

2. Employer plan

If the spouse under 65 is working, then consider whether there are more affordable options through work.

3.   Public Marketplace

With the Affordable Care Act, individuals will be able to purchase plans on the ACA exchanges (Federal or State depending on where you live). Individuals with certain income levels can qualify for a tax subsidy to make premiums more affordable. Plans may also be available as a direct purchase from health insurance companies if an individual does not qualify for tax subsidies.

SECTION 5: Saving money

The goal of this section is to highlight some

of the most common ways to save money

with Medicare.

5.1 Part B and D surcharges

If you make more than $85,000 (single) or $170,000 (joint) in adjusted gross income, you'll pay a Part B and Part D surcharge.

How much you pay is a determined by how much you make. There are different tiers based on income (see Section 1).

The surcharges are based on your income looking back 2 years. This means that your surcharge in 2018 would be based on your income in 2016.

Many individuals retire and go on Medicare.

Retirement typically results in a lower annual

income.

In this situation, the Social Security

Administration has a "Life Changing Event" form

SSA-44 for individuals to declare what the

expected income is for the current year and request

an adjustment accordingly. If your income for the

current year is in a lower tier than what it was 2

years ago, then you will be able to get a reduction

in your Part B and Part D surcharges.

You will have to provide some type of proof that

your income has changed whether it is through

income statements or a letter of termination from

your prior employer.

You can find the form on SSA.gov or by

requesting it directly from your local Social

Security office.

5.2 Dental

Medicare typically does not cover routine dental care or procedures.

Most dental plans will cover you for two cleanings, a set of x-rays, and one exam. Some will cover you for minor procedures such as fillings and extractions, while the more robust plans will cover you for major procedures such as root canals, crowns, and bridges.

Dental plans typically have a benefit cap of between $1000-$1500, meaning once the insurance company pays out that amount, you're on your own.

For retirees, we see three major options to access dental care:

1. Buy a traditional dental insurance plan

This option is great for individuals who get their routine cleanings and may need the occasional procedure (fillings etc.) on a yearly basis.

2. Pay cash

Some dentists will give a senior discount and the degree of discount is based on each individual dentist. Ask your dentist what his or her discount would be. Often times, if someone is just getting 2 cleanings and checkup every year, it may be worthwhile to pay cash and put the difference in the bank.

3. Dental discount programs

Dental discount programs are similar to a BJ's or Costco memberships where you pay a yearly fee to get an across the board discount on dental services. These programs could save you a substantial amount of money on large procedures. Dental discount programs are not insurance and you should ask your dentist if they take these programs.

5.3 State and non-profit assistance programs

Depending on your income, there may be state assistance programs available to help seniors in need.

The programs do vary by state. Some of the most common services available are:

1. Pharmaceutical assistance

Prescription drug costs can greatly affect the quality of life for seniors. Some states may offer programs to assist seniors with high drug costs especially in the donut hole.

2. Transportation

For seniors who are ill, it may be difficult to get around especially to doctor's appointments. There may be services to provide necessary transportation for day-to-day needs as well as doctor appointments.

3. Food and heating

It is important to stay nourished and warm for good health (I know I'm stating the obvious here). For seniors who cannot make ends meet, there are programs available to offset the cost of food and comfort.

4. Low income subsidies (LIS)

Some individuals with low income could qualify for special assistance for their Part B premiums as well as coverage for their prescription co-pays. For more information on these programs, contact Social Security and ask about the Extra Help Program.

For a list of available program and to see whether you qualify, visit your local senior center or contact your local Department of Elderly Affairs.

5.4 Pharmaceutical grants

Unfortunately, drug discount programs typically do not work with Medicare.

For individuals with rare chronic conditions requiring specialty prescriptions, there may be some relief.

Specialty prescriptions are typically in the top tiers. Many individuals with specialty medications will fall into the donut hole within the first few months of the year and can come out of the donut hole in a few short months as well.

Makers of certain specialty prescriptions understand that the high cost can be prohibitive to care. There are grants available from the pharmaceutical companies to assist individuals based on income and other need criteria. To see if your situation qualifies you for a grant, contact the patient assistance program at the pharmaceutical company that makes your prescriptions.

Often times, the need is not only based on income, but sometimes factors such as how long you've been on the drug and circumstances related to your health can apply.

5.5 Paying cash for prescriptions

Not all prescription plans are created equally.

Some plans cover a larger portion of brand name

medications while some other ones cover generics

at a lower cost.

Especially for generics, the cash prices can vary

significantly between drug plans. This is because

each prescription plan negotiates a different price

with each pharmacy chain.

In some cases, paying cash for your generics may

be less expensive than paying your share of the

negotiated price under your insurance plan.

A chat with your local pharmacist about the insurance cost versus cash price of your prescriptions can lead to great savings.

Many pharmacies also have drug discount programs where generics are discounted to an amount lower than co-pays. This would not only offer savings on generics but prevents the costs of generics from affecting your coverage gap calculations.

Another way to purchase your medications for cash is overseas. Typically if you go to a country such as Canada, you'll need to have a written prescription by a Canadian Licensed Physician.

However, other overseas pharmacies will accept U.S. Prescriptions. There's no guarantee that the manufacturer will be the same as in-state. Make sure to verify with the foreign country's licensure site to make sure that the pharmacy you're buying from is licensed.

5.6 Comparing different pharmacies and mail order

Each drug plan will give you the option of ordering your prescriptions via mail order instead of picking it up at the pharmacy. The mail order program is through a preferred company that the prescription plan has contracts with (or owns) and may often lead to greater savings.

Some plans will also have preferred pharmacies versus non-preferred pharmacies. Preferred pharmacies will give a bigger discount on co-pays versus non-preferred pharmacies. Savings could be upwards of 10-20% on average when you use a preferred pharmacy.

5.7 Payment programs

Especially for Advantage plans, sometimes out of pocket expenses can be too much of a financial burden.

Two of the biggest areas we see for large medical bills are:

- **Hospitalizations**

Many Advantage plans and some supplemental plans require significant out of pocket expenses if you get hospitalized. Advantage plans may require daily co-pays and certain supplemental plans may require you to pay for the Part A deductible ($1316 for 2017).

- **Outpatient procedures**

Some plans require a co-insurance on outpatient procedures. Unlike co-pays, which are a set dollar amount, co-insurances are a percentage of total costs.

For example, a co-insurance of 20% on a $5,000 procedure will cost you $1,000 in out of pocket expenses.

For some, a thousand dollar bill may be too much to handle all at once. Luckily, most providers and hospitals will arrange for a payment plan where you can pay in monthly installments until your bill is paid off without affecting your credit.

Ask your provider or hospital's billing department about these types of payment plans if you're in a situation where you cannot afford your bills.

5.8 Formulary Exceptions and denied claims

The prescription plan you chose is typically based on what prescriptions you're currently on. What happens when a new prescription that's not on your plan's formulary is prescribed or if a current prescription is no longer covered?

In these cases, your plan will typically grant out a trial supply of the medication. However, you can also request a formulary exception from the prescription plan to cover that particular drug for the year.

If your drug is in a higher tier to a point where it is unaffordable, then you can also request a tier exception so that the drug is in a less expensive tier.

You can request exceptions by contacting the prescription plan and coordinating with your prescribing physician.

Sometimes Medicare or your Medicare Advantage plan can deny a service you've received. In certain cases, you may be responsible for the full cost. However, if you feel that the service you've received is medically necessary, you can request for your claim to be reconsidered by Medicare.

Typically you have 120 days to file for an appeal.

For a great summary on how to approach appeals,

visit the CMS website:

https://www.cms.gov/Outreach-and-

Education/Medicare-Learning-Network-

MLN/MLNProducts/downloads/MedicareAppeals

process.pdf

5.9 Medicaid and Medicaid Planning

Medicaid provides assistance to individuals who are low income. Medicaid rules differ in each state but are typically based on income and assets. States calculate Medicaid eligibility based on a percentage of the Federal Poverty Level. To see if you qualify for Medicaid, the best way is to contact your local Medicaid office or senior center.

Individuals who qualify for Medicare and Medicaid are "Dual Eligible." For Dual Eligible individuals, Medicare pays first, and then Medicaid picks up the rest.

Medicaid will pay for Part B premiums, Part D premiums, co-insurance, and co-pays for medical services. Co-pays for prescriptions will also be greatly reduced as well as coverage in the donut hole.

Dual eligible individuals may also qualify for special Advantage plans called Senior Care Options plans that better coordinate Medicare and Medicaid into a single plan. However, not every state offers these special plans.

BONUS SECTION

Now that you understand the basics of

Medicare, I'd like to conclude by sharing the

most effective way to navigate Medicare

yourself (checklist included).

How to (really) navigate Medicare

Start the Medicare process by understanding your needs first. Ignore the ABCDs and the fine print.

Start with your health. Are you healthy or do you suffer from several health conditions? As we have covered, a healthy individual may lean towards Advantage plans, while an unhealthy individual may lean towards a supplemental plan.

Then move onto your lifestyle. Are you planning on staying local or living in multiple states? For the most part, emergencies are covered with any plan regardless of network restrictions so you won't have to worry too much about being covered on trips. If you stay local, Advantage plans may

be a good fit. If you are living in multiple states

and would like a medical team available to you

everywhere you live, then lean towards a

Supplemental Plan (or the very least an Advantage

plan with out of network benefits).

End with the budget. Do you know how much

you can afford and yet be able to live the

retirement you anticipated? Like any other

insurance, more coverage typically means more

money.

Once you have identified your needs, you'll be

able to clearly distinguish between Supplemental

Plan + Part D versus an Advantage Plan.

If you fall into the Supplemental Plan + Part D category:

1. Find the right letter plan to match your needs (we recommend you take a look at F, G, or N).

2. Compare prices between the same letter plans (be sure to take a look at the history of rate increases as well).

3. Find the right Part D plan using the Medicare.gov website by putting in your prescriptions and pharmacy.

If you fall into the Advantage category:

1. Make sure your doctors are covered.

2. Make sure your prescriptions are covered.

3. Pay attention to the co-pays especially for

hospital stays and outpatient procedures.

Shopping for a plan:

There are numerous resources to help you navigate your options. The most common are:

Insurance companies

By calling a particular insurance company, a representative from that company will walk you through the available choices from only that company. However, theses individuals are typically very well versed on that company's plans.

SHIP Counselors

State Health Insurance Assistance Program provides free state funded support to navigate individuals through their Medicare options. SHIP counselors are typically well trained on the ins and outs of Medicare, but may not be able to help you with issues that may arise between you and the insurance company after or during enrollment.

Independent insurance agents

Independent agents work typically with numerous insurance companies and are compensated via commission for enrollments. However, Independent insurance agents may not work with all the available options and may be looking to sell you other non-Medicare related insurance.

Independent consultants

Independent consultants charge a fee to help you navigate Medicare. These individuals may be more hands on counselors in terms of customer service and will offer you an unbiased comparison.

Start the Medicare process 2-3 months before you need coverage to begin.

Your Checklist

- ✓ Sign up for Parts A + B through social security
- ✓ Sign up a Supplemental + Part D or and Advantage plan
- ✓ Wait for your cards to arrive in the mail in approximately 2-3 weeks

ABOUT DR. JOHN LUO AND DOCTOR'S CHOICE

Dr. John Luo started Doctor's Choice in 2013 out of frustration from the lack of concise education and guidance for patients transitioning to Medicare. Prior to Doctor's Choice, Dr. Luo was involved in academic research in the fields of holistic and regenerative medicine with over 16 manuscripts in respected peer-review academic Journals.

At Doctor's Choice, we focus on providing unbiased guidance on Supplemental, Advantage, and Part D Prescription plans. We offer customized seminars for employers and individual consultations for retirees. We have the goal of navigating one million Americans through Medicare by 2020.

For more information or to request a consultation or seminar, please visit us at www.DoctorsChoiceUSA.com

Made in the USA
Columbia, SC
20 March 2018